they lit fires

lenti hatch o yog

Monologues, Haibun and Songs.

by

Raine Geoghegan

First published 2019 by The Hedgehog Poetry Press

Published in the UK by
The Hedgehog Poetry Press
Coppack House, 5
Churchill Avenue
Clevedon
BS21 6QW

www.hedgehogpress.co.uk

ISBN: 978-1-9160908-2-8

A CIP Catalogue record for this book is available from the British
Library.

Gypsy Romanies have been sitting round the fire for hundreds of years. At the end of the day they come together, share stories, talk things through, sing songs and sometimes just sit in the quiet of the night. They carry the fire in their hearts. These monologues, haibun and songs remind us of the power of story, of reflecting on the lives that have been and gone.

I dedicate this collection of poems to my daughter Rebecca Norris and my son Luke Geoghegan, my strength and joy, and for all those who lit fires

'I love the fire as my own heart.'

Bronislawa Wajs, known as Papusza, Polish Romany classic poet and singer
-17.08.08 - 8.02.87

'I was born on the road when me mother was 'awkin' pegs and I've bin a roamin' Gypsy since I learned to use me legs I can catch me self a rabbit I can catch me self a hare a partridge or a pheasant I can catch most anywhere.'

Jean Smith, a Romany woman and member of the Romany Heritage and Family History Society. May 30th 2019.

Contents

BONES 'N' SPOONS

before I played the spoons
I played the bones
before I played the bones
I listened
to me father
playing the spoons
to me granda
playing the bones
and as I tell you this
me son is listenin'
the bones, they are a waitin'
and the spoons, well they're in the kitchen drawer.

UNDER A GOOSEBERRY BUSH

im john ripley

somewhere in kent, this is where I was borned and laid in me mother's arms,
crying for me dear life. it was a warm day in june, me mum and 'er people
were on their way to the 'op fields in peasmarsh. me dad 'ad gone ahead to
meet some mushes, don't ask. me poor mum was findin' it 'ard, 'er carryin' me
near to 'er time and the bump, bump, bump of the wheels of the vardo.

they stopped in the poove to 'ave some 'obben, aunt may was makin' joey gray,
the chavies were runnin' around. me mum was soakin' 'er feet in cool water.
that's when it started, 'er waters broke and the bowl went flyin', there was
'ollerin' and shoutin', aunt may moved me mum under the bushes, told me
cousin to get 'elp from another travelling family. it was touch and go, according
to me bein' the wrong way round but thank the lord there was a rackley who
'ad delivered a lot of chavies, she pulled me out and I was borned.

I was named john ripley, after me dad. the 'ead rom came down and blessed me,
ee tied a little bag of rowan berries round me neck to ward off the bad mulo and
to bring kushtie bok. all the rackley's put a little coin in me 'and, as was the custom.
luckily me aunt and uncle 'ad left patrin signs along the way so we 'ad plenty of
folk to wet me little 'ead. it's not everyday a chavi gets borned under a gooseberry
bush. 'course I never 'eard the end of it, me mum and dad teased me rotten and when I te
folks they don't believe it, mind you, it set me up fer life, gave me strength and I've
'ad a bloody kushtie life, I can tell yer. me mum used to tell me this story over and over,
to tell yer the truth I've loved tellin' it as much as 'earing it.

*Romani words: Vardo - wagon. Poove - field. Hobben - food. Chavies - children. Head
Rom - Gypsy elder. Rackleys - women. Patrin - leaves that were tied up and left on trees or
by the roadside to let family know which way the wagons went.*

THE GUVENY – A HAIBUN

Harry leans against the brick wall in the alleyway, smoking a roll-up. His black stadi pulled down, almost covering his right eye. He wears a navy and white pinstripe suit. Anyone would think he was off to the city, but no, he's taking five to prepare himself for the meeting with his parole officer. He's planning on getting there early and making a good impression.

Just as he's finishing his smoke a brown cow walks into the garden, eyes like coal, calm as you like. Harry looks up, wonders if he's dreaming.

> With nostrils flared
> breath rising into cold air,
> the brown cow bellows.

'Well, I'll be blowed, it's a bloomin' guveney.' He says.

A guerro runs down the road, stops at Harry's gate, shouts to another guerro who's marching briskly behind.

'It's alright Jim, he's here.'

Harry drops his cigarette butt, stamps on it with his right foot. He walks up to the cow.

'Aint you a kushti guveney? Where did you come from then?'

The guerro tells him that the cow wandered off from the field near the reservoir.

'We'll be getting him back now mate, sorry for any inconvenience.'

Harry shrugs his shoulders, strokes the creature's head.

> The cow stands erect
> appears rooted to the spot,
> oblivious to men.

Harry watches the men lead the animal away. He thinks this will be a good topic of conversation to share with his probation officer, keep the mood light.

Romani words: Guveney – cow; Stadi – trilby hat; Guerro – man; Kushti – good.

ON THE TOBER WITH LOOLLADI

Every Friday and Saturday Granny was up early tying bunches of loolladi then putting them on her cart. She wore a paisley scarf, a dark blue money belt with a side pocket round her waist, gold earrings and a gold sovereign on a chain at her neck. I liked to sit on the back doorstep and watch her, she tied them with a type of string called bass. When it got wet it frayed and smelled of Weetabix. She worked swiftly, rhythmically and when all the flowers were on the cart she stood back, admiring them as if she was looking at a work of art. My favourites were dahlias, deep purples, soft reds, bright orange.I also loved sweet peas. Sometimes Granny would give me one to put on my pillow. I remember once falling asleep smelling the lovely scent.

I would open the gate for her, in my pyjamas. The familiar sound of the wheels rolling over the drain in the alleyway made me think of trains.

'Bye my gel, see to Granfaver, won't yer?'

'Alright Granny.' I'd reply.

On her return in the late afternoon, her cart empty, her face glowing. She'd say.

'Alf, make me a cup of mesci, I'm parched.'

While Grandfather was making her tea she would untie the money belt, count out
her poshes. I'd kneel on the floor and watch her place the coins and notes in piles.

Then she'd say.

'The Lord's good, but I ain't arf dukkering'.

Into my hands she'd drop some coins.

'Right now, let's get the 'obben on'.

That night we'd have a proper feast, lamb chops, mashed potatoes, ham and piccalilli, carrots and peas, fresh crusty bread or the left over Joey Gray that Grandfather loved. Sometimes we had fresh strawberries from Kent and whipped cream.

When we finished eating, we'd flop on the sofa and armchairs for a while and watch telly, I'd help Granny to wash up. Grandfather, well he'd go for a walk and a smoke, I could smell it on his breath when he kissed me goodnight. Sometimes I would teach Granny a new word, writing it down so she could copy letter for letter. The curtains pulled, doors locked. I would go to bed and fall asleep listening to Grandfather playing a lullaby on his harmonica.

Romani words: Tober - road; Loolladi - flowers; Mesci - tea; Dukkering - aching; Obben - dinner.

THE GREENHOUSE

Mourners spill out into the alleyway. Amidst the black
are flashes of purple and red of women's scarves and
men's ties.

My uncle, a staff sergeant in the army and just back from
Germany is dressed in his uniform. He leans against the
kitchen wall, having a smoke. We drink tea laced with
whiskey. My aunts dry their tears on freshly pressed white
handkerchiefs.

I go into the sitting room and see my sister sitting on a stool,
her hands clasped tightly on her lap. The coffin is open.
Grandfather is in his best suit. His pocket watch hangs from
his top pocket. A family photograph is tucked into his waistcoat
close to his heart. His old hip flask lies at his side, no doubt
there will be a little whiskey in there. He still wears his gold ring.
He looks as if he's resting, as if he'll sit up at any moment.
I place my hand gently on his ...

*Grandfather and I are walking down the path to the green
house. I am six years old. It's a hot day, I'm wearing my
shorts. Weeds and wildflowers tickle my ankles. He pushes
the door open, ushers me in, points upwards. 'What d'ya think
of the grapes my gal?' Tilting my head back I see huge bunches,
deep red, ready to be plucked. He reaches up, pulls a few
down, rinses them in a bowl of water then places them in
my hand. I bite one and the juice runs down my chin.
I eat two more. 'They're lovely Grandfather'. He smiles,
opens a can of beer, takes a mouthful and say's. 'Do ya see
these grapes? Do ya know why they're so tasty?' I shake
my head. 'Well it's because the Mulo watches over 'em.'
He laughs, I laugh but I'm not sure who the Mulo is.*

I finish my cup of tea and tell granny that I am going down
to the greenhouse. The door is slightly ajar, the white paint
faded, flaking. I push the door hard, go in and smell sawdust,
stale beer and decay.There is an open can of Pale Ale on the
shelf, alongside three broken brown pots. An old knife with
a blue handle, its blade stuck in the wood. It's the one he used
to carve the wagons with. I bend down; pull an old crate out
and in front of me the unfinished wagon. Taking a tissue from my
pocket I wipe the dust off. It's painted red, green and yellow.
Tiny faded net curtains hang limply against the small windows.
The front door has minute horseshoes attached to it. All the
Romany's believe them to bring good luck. I would love to
have this wagon. Before I leave I look up to where the grapes
used to grow in abundance. All that is left is a dried, tangled
vine hanging loosely from the roof.

Romani word: Mulo - spirit of the ancestors.

KORING CHIRICLO I – A TRIOLET

When the Romany's were forced off the roads into houses they were
saddened by the fact that they could no longer hear the cuckoo sing.

I've loved to hear the cuckoo sing.
I'm a Romany, always travelling
from Huntingdon to King's Lyn.
I've loved to hear the cuckoo sing
since I was a chavi in a sling.
Summer, autumn, winter, ah spring.
I've loved to hear the cuckoo sing.
I'm a Romany. Always travelling.

Romani words: Koring Chiriclo – a cuckoo; Chavi - a child.

KORING CHIRICLO II – A TRIOLET

Jel on me dad would say.
Pack up yer covels, we'll be on our way.
Take our time, get to Frome's 'ill by May.
Jel on, me dad would say.
The cuckoo's callin', untie the grai,
up onto the vardo. It's a kushti day.
Jel on, me dad would say.
Pack up yer covels. We'll be on our way.

*Romani words. Koring Chiriclo - a cuckoo; Jel on - move on; Covels -
belongings; Grai - horses; Vardo - wagons; Kushti - lovely.*

THE POOKERING KOSH - THE TALKING STICK

Me granda is dyin'.
We're packed tight inside the vardo.
'*Dik at the old guerro,*' Me cousin say's.
'E aint long fer this world.' Well. We all jin that.
I'm crouching by the door when an ole' mush
comes in carryin' a stick of blackthorn.
'*Ere's the pookering kosh.*' Me granny say's.
She picks up the youngest, our Emily and puts 'er on the bed.
The ole' mush gives the kosh to me granda, who can barely 'old it.
Me granny takes the chavies vast and squeezes the other end of the kosh
into 'er little fingers.
Everyone is quiet.
The mush sings a gillie, well it's more like diddlin to me'.
Me granda lifts 'is 'ead, smiles at Emily then falls back wiv a gasp.
No one moves. I'm 'oldin' me breath.
The chavi takes the kosh and waves it in the air.
Me granny say's. '*That's right our gel, we jin what you're doin'*.
She laughs then roves, one by one they rove until
they're all at it and I breathe out.
I whispers to me cousin, '*Come on, let's jel and play in the poove.*'
We get out of that vardo quick sharp, we leave 'em to it.

*Romani words: Vardo - wagon; Dik - look; Guerro - man; Jin - to know; Mush
- man; chavi - child; Vast - hand; Gillie - song; Diddlin - singing diddiley dee's;
Roves - weeps; Jel - come on; Poove - field. It is the custom in some Romany
families ,that when an elder dies a ritual is practised using the blackthorn stick as
a way to pass on wisdom and knowledge from that elder to a small child.*

O LILLAI GILLIE

(Angloromani)

Prey o lillai, prey o lillai
Gillyava a gillie
Prey o chick, prey o charos
Gillyava a gillie

Prey a panni, prey o panni
Gillyava a gillie
Shoon me vas' tacha
Gillyava a gillie

Prey o raddi, prey o raddi
Gillyava a gillie
Chumos for me pen
Gillyava a gillie

Prey o lillai, prey o lillai
Gillyava a gillie
Prey o chick, prey o charos
Gilyava a gillie

Gillyava a gillie, gillyava a gillie
Shoon me vas tatcha,
Gillyava a gillie

DIRTY LITTLE FLOWER GIRL

us gypsy chavies 'ad it 'ard in the days when we 'ad to go to school. the giorgios used to ca us names, they spat on us, told tales, but we were there to learn, it's what our mothers and fathers wanted. i'd rather 'ave been out on the tober, travelling around England, although will say I'm pleased that I 'ad an education of sorts, it 'elped me to get on in life and I've '. some kushti jobs.

me sister and I went to the local school, we 'ad a lot of time off for travelling. I can't say th I liked it there; well I would 'ave done if we weren't all cooped up like chickens, sometimes I felt like I couldn't breathe. i didn't like mrs frances, me teacher then again, she didn't like me. one lunchtime I was standing in the line waiting to get me 'obben, she shouted at me.

'You're holding the queue up, move along, be quick.'

l moved along but I 'eard her say to another teacher.

'dirty little flower girl.'

somethin' snapped inside me 'ead and I said, without thinkin'.

'I'm not dirty.'

she looked at me, fierce like, her face turning red. she put 'er vast out, bent down and slapped me legs, 'ard. i didn't cry, just moved along the line to get me 'obben.

me dad picked me up from school, I was very quiet all the way home. Me mum gave me a cuddle and a kiss when we got in, she smelled of roses which was nice compared to the smell of steak and onions that she'd been cookin'. after dinner she undressed me to me vest and knickers, I sat on the draining board, as she started to wash me legs she called out.

'arry, come 'ere, dik at the baby's legs.'

he asked me how I got the bruises, I wouldn't say. he said.

'dordi, dordi 'as somebody snoped yer?'

I cried but still didn't tell them. it was ages until I finally did.

the next morning she marched me to school. we went straight to the 'ead teacher's office. I 'ad to wait in the corridor, there was a strong smell of polish. I sat there for ages, I saw mrs frances go in, on the wall in front of me was a picture of the rounders team, I thought I'd like to be in that team, they all looked 'appy and friendly. after a while me teacher came out, walking fast, looking down at 'er feet. me mum came out. She grabbed me 'and, took me to the class room. she said.

'it's done and sorted, now go and learn my babe.'

i never did find out what 'appened in that office, i 'ad a good guess. i was at that school for another year but the teacher never bothered me again. i never did get to be in the rounder's team though.

Romani words: Chavies – children; Giorgios – Non Romany; Tober – road; Kushti – very good; Dik – look; Dordi dordi – Oh my goodness; Snoped – hit.

A ROMANY GUERRO REMEMBERS

Facebook 27 December 2016

'i remember me uncle nassy lee living in a bow top vardo, it was on a grass verge in a lane called bonus lane in crewe he 'ad seven or eight children an' i used to visit wiv me other cousins bobby and taylor boy me uncle nassy was me grannies brother her maiden name was smith I'd love to 'ere from any of 'em.' RT.

Facebook 28 December 2016

'there was a traveller woman her name was sally lee she 'ad one eye and a son called money, she used to go 'awking with 'er trushnie filled wiv combs, pegs, old silver and lucky 'eather, i think she used to live around the pottery area of stoke – all the best.' RT.

Facebook 30 December 2016

'it's nice to 'ear from you raine – the 'op pickin' i done is at a place in hertfordshire called rimal – we used to stay in little cabins wiv straw on the floor that me mum made up into a bed, me dad was a pole puller he pulled the 'op vines down, we 'ad a crib and we used to strip the 'ops from the vine then put 'em all in the crib, you got paid by the bushel – a basket filled to the top worked out to a bushel, i used to go in the dryin' kilns, they dried the 'ops and they smelled of sulphur – it smelled strong – you mention rokkerin in romani, well apart from a few words i've long forgotten the language – me mum and dad spoke it all the time but since they passed none of us speak it i did 'ave a few pages of different words that me sister gave me but it's in a drawer somewhere. You're better to look on the internet i bet there's lots of sites where you'll find it all the best RT'

Romani words: Geurro – man; Vardo – wagon; Hawking - selling; Trushnie - hawking basket; Rokkerin – speaking; Jib – language.

UP EARLY, HAIBUN

She walks the three mile journey in all weathers, pushing her empty barrow through the station yard. Burt the Guard, is always there to greet her, he lost a hand in the trenches and she calls him a *'dear, blessed man.'* Dressed in her green pinafore and coat, her side pocket tied around her waist, and wearing a purple head scarf, she sucks peppermints.

Pushing her barrow up the ramp she enters the carriage at the end of the train, standing all the way from Feltham to Waterloo. Once there, she walks swiftly out of the station and over Waterloo Bridge then onto Nine Elms market where she buys the freshest, most colourful loolladi. This is where she uses cunning to get what she wants, never paying the full price. She bumps into *'all sorts of characters.'* There's Joey who runs the café who gives her tips on the horses. There's old Mrs Kray who sells tulips when they're in season, a relative of sorts.

> Spanish dancers
> blood orange dahlias
> soaking in water.

'Ooh, yer can't beat 'em.' She also loves carnations. *'ow much do yer want fer these cars?'* The seller says, *'Two pounds for you Amy.'* *'I'll give yer one pound fifty and not a penny more and I'll 'ave another two boxes.'* He tries charging her more but she's not having it. She walks away, he calls her back. *'Alright Amy, they're yours'.'* The barrow is filled box by box, she ties them tight with string then says, *'I'm off 'ome.'* By the time she gets home to 'anarth, she's worn out. A bowl of oxtail, a drop of whiskey and she's ready for bed. Her husband wraps his arms around her waist. She says. *'Go to sleep Alf, I'm dukkered.'*

Romani words (jib): Kushti – very good; Lolladi – flowers; Dukkered – exhausted.

GREAT AUNT TILDA, A FUNNY OLD MALT

me great aunt tilda, now there was a character, a funny old malt. she was me dad's aunt on the lane side of the family. she always wore men's clothes, dark coloured trousers, shirts, waistcoats, a black stadi with a gold 'at pin on the side and a little purple feather. she smoked a swiggler, her fingers yellowed from nicotine. she carried a carpet bag wherever she went, inside a flask of strong black tea with a little drop of panni in it. she'd refuse anyone else's tea, sayin', *'yer never know what they put in it.'* she spoke in a deep voice. when she got in a temper it grew deeper, us gels would be frit to death.

every friday night she'd go the brown bear, 'ave a few drinks with the family, often getting skimmished and if granny amy was there she'd end up fightin' and cursin'. the men would 'ave to pull 'er off me granny, they just couldn't get on, those two. before she went 'ome, she'd shout out. *'i've 'ad enough of this place, I'm goin' 'ome to get a sooti.'* she'd walk all the way 'ome, over seven miles. she never would get on a bus, didn't matter 'ow far she 'ad to go.

when she turned sixty, she packed up 'er covels and went to the care 'ome in shepperton, phil common it was called. we all thought it strange but she said that she didn't want to be a burden on anyone. she still went calling and did 'er little bit of shoppin' but that was 'er 'ome until she died, I think it was some eighteen years later. she'd never married, said she was 'appy without an 'usband. sometimes, she told jokes and rokkered a lot in romani, 'rokker more romanes', she'd say.

if someone was ill or grievin', she'd say, *'I'll burn a bit've salt for 'em.'* If someone got in a car or did something adventurous, she'd say *'if yer goes and kills yerself, don't come back and blame me.'* me dad always spoke of 'er but he used to make us laugh when he said, *'our tilda's a funny old malt, always's 'as been, always's will be.'*

Romani words:
Stadi – trilby hat, panni – brandy, swiggler – pipe, calling – buying and selling clothes, rokkered – spoke, skimmished, tipsy/drunk. malt – woman, sootti – a good sleep

THEY LIT FIRES, MOVED IN CLOSE

dikka kie my carrie come and sit yerself down

yer look dukkered

me granny used to sit by the yog all the time

rubbing 'er 'ands then movin' 'em close to the flames

'er skin turned dark and she said that the fire did it

dark raddi's with no moon

only the brightness of the yog

great aunt bethy tellin' a story
the one about 'er great great granny Margret
who drowned in a ditch drunk as a lord
her face down in the water
'alf a dozen piglets running around and over 'er,
them not seemin' to notice

'ands 'olding saucers of mesci with drops of tatti-panni in 'em

all of the malts slowly gettin' skimmished

Romani words: dikka kie – look here; dukkered – done in; yog – fire; raddi's –
nights; Mesci – tea; tatti-panni – brandy; malts – women; skimmished – drunk.

APPENDIX: ENGLISH TRANSLATION
OF O LILLAI GILLIE

The Summer Song

In the summer, in the summer
I will sing a song
Of the earth, of the heavens
I will sing a song

On the river, on the river
I will sing a song
Listen my beloved
I will sing a song

In the night, in the night
I will sing a song
Kisses for my love
I will sing a song

In the summer, in the summer
I will sing a song
Of the earth, of the heavens
I will sing a song

I will sing a song, a song
Listen my beloved,
I will sing a song

IN APPRECIATION

I would like to thank the following people for their support and encouragement: my husband Simon who is always there for me; my cousin Julie for her input with 'dirty little flower girl'; Tara Sutherland for her research into the Ripley Family; Christine Ford for her stunning artwork; Mark at Hedgehog Poetry Press for publishing this work; James Simpson, my mentor and friend; Isaac Blake at Romani Arts. Thanks also to the Creative Writing team at University of Chichester and especially to friends Naomi Foyle, Zoe Mitchell, Brenda Bayne and Hannah Brockbank, Lillian Howan, Francis Reilly and the Travellers' Times. Finally to the Hedgehog poets for their support and friendship.

ACKNOWLEDGMENTS

Many thanks to the editors of the following publications in which these poems have previously been published: *Under a Gooseberry Bush*, The Clearing/Little Toller Publishing, (September 2018); *The Guveney*, The Clearing/Little Toller Publishing,(May 2019); *O Lillie Gillie*, Poethead, (March 2019); *On the Tober with Loolladi*, The Travellers' Times, (December 2018); *The Greenhouse*, Poetry Ireland Review, (December 2018); *Koring Chiriclo I*, The Clearing/Little Toller Publishing, (September 2018*); Koring Chiriclo II* Under the Radar, (Summer 2018); *Dirty Little Flower Girl*, The Travellers' Times, (February 2018); *Great Aunt Tilda*, The Ofi Press, (October 2018); *Up Early*, The Narrow Road, (August 2019).

The following monologues can be heard on Soundcloud: 'Under a Gooseberry Bush', 'Koring Chiriclo I' and ' The Guveney', available on podcast at www.littletoller.co.uk/the-clearing/new-poetry-by-raine-geoghegan

PRAISE FOR THEY LIT FIRES : LENTI HATCH O YOG

"They lit fires: lenti hatch o yog' is a bright kaleidoscope collection of monologues, triolets, haibun and songs. Each is a vignette that tells a story of a disappearing Romany way of life. Raine Geoghegan has captured fleeting moments and expressed them in a language that rings sharp and true. Like the best storytellers, she has created characters who will live long in the reader's memory."

- Debjani Chatterjee, MBE, FRSA. Award winning poet.

"The Travellers' Times is always pleased and proud to publish Raine's popular and evocative prose and poetry on our website and in our magazine. We have a range of readers, Gypsy, Roma, Travellers and Gorja. Raine's work manages to reach out of the page and touches the hearts of all of them. We thoroughly recommend 'they lit fires: lenti hatch o yog' to anyone who is not familiar with Raine's work. To those who are already familiar – no recommendation will be needed."

- Mike Doherty, Editor, Travellers' Times.

"Raine Geoghegan's poetry is like stepping inside another world. Gently she guides you through her culture with word visions with much beauty"'

- Jess Smith, Scottish Author and Storyteller.

PRAISE FOR APPLE WATER: POVEL PANNI

"These are poems of Roma memory and survival brought to life through beguiling lyric and dramatic telling. They bring a way of living, of thinking, listening, and seeing into immediate and natural focus."

- David Morley, winner of the Ted Hughes Award for New Poetry. (2018)

"Raine Geoghegan's very atmospheric Hedgehog Poetry Press pamphlet Apple Water: Povel Panni has brought a sense of summer back to the currently grey-near winter days and reminds me of so many things I personally would hate the world to lose. The poems are lush and warm with sounds, language and the sense of important family, nature and Romany tradition."

- S.A. Leavesley, Poet. (2018)

"Geoghegan writes knowingly about the essential things in life: work, food, shelter and clothing. She homes in on the importance of things that bring a family together: work in the fields picking fruit, vegetables and hops, meal times and songs."

- Neil Leadbeater, Write Out Loud.

"Raine Geoghegan's lovely elegiac pamphlet from Hedgehog Press was, as its dually linguistic title suggest, full of poems using both English and Romany language (jib). The poems with a gentle, matter of fact tone delivered such emotional depth and resonance. The poems were alive with humour, memory and moments of loss. I adored the vibrant characters from Geoghegan's family; her Grandmother's love of strong tea and memorable phrases; 'you've mullered (killed) it", she says of dropped pet tortoise; Uncle Tommy Ripley with his armful of flowers ("loolladi") and the author's Mother, travelled back in time: 'I see you smiling/ I hear you say/ Daddy, Daddy, wait for me.' (I See You in the Hop Fields).

- Deborah Tyler-Bennett, Under the Radar.